Your Guide to a Perfect Fashion Show Production

By MsNickee Mack
Foreword by Gwen Devoe

Copyright © 2016 by MsNickee Mack

All rights reserved. No part of this publication may be reproduced, distributed, or transmitted in any form or by any means, including photocopying, recording, or other electronic or mechanical methods, without the prior written permission of the publisher, except in the case of brief quotations embodied in critical reviews and certain other noncommercial uses permitted by copyright law. For permission requests, write to the publisher, addressed "Attention: Permissions Coordinator," at the email address below:

Ganny Pie Media & Publishing
info@gannypie.com
www.gannypie.com

Quantity sales. Special discounts are available on quantity purchases by corporations, associations, trade bookstores, wholesalers and others. For details, contact the publisher at the address above.

Printed in the United States of America
First printing, 2015
ISBN-13: 978-1535474108

TABLE OF CONTENTS

Foreword 1

Introduction 3

Theme ... Cause ... Time 6

Your Venue 10

Your Designers 15

Models ... Casting Call ...Casting Call Location 19

The Host 24

Videography/Photography 29

Entertainment 31

Backstage Manager Front-of-House Ticketmaster Front-of-House Floor Manager 33

You Have to Pay to Play 46

Just So You Know 48

Resources 55

About the Author 107

Foreword

What do you do when you have personally met and experienced the works of a *Producer's producer?* Most times you sit, smile and revel in the fact that it's not your event and it's not your headache; but, watching MsNickee in action is a totally different experience. You want to assist her as she works tirelessly to deliver what she has promised. Poised, confident and assertive, MsNickee—more often than not—over delivers. I have been a producer of many, many events and fashion shows over the last 20 years. However, in 2009 with my creation and the ultimate launch of Full Figured Fashion Week®, I earned the title of an Executive Producer. What is the difference? Mainly, the amount of delegation that is required, the size of your team and the size of your production budget. Overseeing a production is tedious. It involves late nights, early mornings, carrying a mobile device in one hand and a contract in the other hand. However, in an industry that was formerly dominated by men, production has taken on a new face, one that I have known for more than 10 years and have watched mature. That face is beat for the Gods, is often layered with soft curls or silky straight, shaded in the latest trend in eyewear and most certainly rocking a purple lip. Yes, it's the *Producer's producer*, MsNickee Mack, CEO of Diva Day International.

I am sure the gems found between these pages will not only inspire and encourage potential fashion show producers, but it will also provide a wealth of education and resources that you don't have to research yourself.

Congrats on your first book, MsNickee, and may we be blessed with the birth of many sequels!

Gwendolyn L. DeVoe
CEO, DeVoe Signature Events, Inc.
Creator & Executive Pro Producer Full Figured Fashion Week®

Introduction

Heyyy Fashion Family,

Lets "chat and chew" briefly before I get into "brewing all this tea!"

First things first—If you desire to put together a show in order to "get rich," let's dismiss that right now! Your first show is to build your network, solidify your brand, build solid professional relationships, document your journey, and develop your target market. If you break even, that's a good thing because to *make* money you have to *spend* money and *spend smart*! If you want this to be an annual event, trademark your name. You will thank me later when your brand becomes popular and successful and someone tries to steal it!!

Please don't go in trying to get everything for free, because you get what you pay for—REMEMBER THAT!! Stay positive throughout the process because it will challenge your nerves; however, as long as you believe in your brand, believe that you can do this.

Now, I truly want to have this conversation with all of you so that you will understand the process of putting on a successful show. I come from a modeling and producing background with a special affinity towards models and producers, so I am actually speaking *directly* to you in some of these chapters, giving you some major tips that you would usually have to take my class to receive. Models: I care about you winning and understanding this industry as a whole, and it includes production! If you are aware of what is required to put together a successful event, you won't be surprised by anything, and this means you *stay ready, so you don't have to get ready*. Always be prepared! Producers: We should adopt the mentality of always being able to learn from one another. What we don't know isn't impossible to find out. Be willing to ask questions. Making this your business requires that you keep an open mind and be not afraid to take risks! My goal with this book is that it be a continued resource for you—a reference guide to help you keep track of your ideas and progress. Use it in conversation. This is what I do when I participate in or put on a production of my own.

The people who have collaborated with me in writing this book are professional entrepreneurs in the hair, beauty and fashion communities and they have worked with me for years and/or have been in my productions. They know my work ethic and they recognize my talent. These folks are EXPERTS in their fields! Now, that having been said . . . let's do this!!

Your Guide to a Perfect Fashion Show Production

The first thing I want to say before we get started, and PLEASE take these words as "gospel" because they are the most profound words you need to remember:

HAVE A BUDGET . . . for EVERYTHING!

Now, let's make a quick checklist . . .

YOUR EVENT NEEDS:

- VENUE
- HOST
- MODELS
- BACKSTAGE/FRONT OF HOUSE COORDINATION
- VENUE TICKETMASTER
- THEME/CAUSE
- MAKEUP ARTISTS
- HAIR STYLISTS
- ENTERTAINMENT
- CASTING
- CASTING LOCATION
- DESIGNERS
- VIDEOGRAPHY/PHOTOGRAPHY
- DJ
- RUNWAY SET UP
- DRESSING ROOM SETUP
- MEDIA
- VENDORS
- CORE TEAM

Not necessarily in that order. This is simply your personal to-do list! You will reorganize these as you read along!

Theme ... Cause ... Time

Y ou are sitting in your office or around the kitchen table with friends and you are discussing your brand (you should have one ... a brand, that is ... if you are putting on any type of production) and you are brainstorming on how to get your name out there ... so you come up with a FASHION SHOW. Now, say this to yourself: WHY, WHAT FOR, and WHEN? Always consider the time of day you want to hold your event, never too early or too late in the day! Examples: Prime times, Friday Late Night Themed Event, Saturday Night Outing Event, Sunday Brunch Show. Let's break those down with some additional details.

A Friday Night Themed Event could be an All-White Party, Work-Week Wine Down, Friday Night Masquerade or a Fashion Fridays series with prizes for best dressed.

A Saturday Night Outing Event could be a Saturday Night Sex-in-the-City event, Saturday Day-Sexy-Singles event, or a Saturday Girl's-Night-Out event.

Your Guide to a Perfect Fashion Show Production

Sunday is always a nice day to have a brunch event: Poolside Parlay, Sunday Fashion Fun Day event. Now, let's discuss your WHY, WHAT FOR, and WHEN.

WHY?

- To build brand recognition
- To bring people together
- To bring about awareness of a specific cause
- To be able to donate to a charity, etc.

WHAT FOR?

- Breast Cancer
- Domestic Violence
- Brand Launch
- Charitable Organization
- Specific Cause, etc.

WHEN?

- What time of year
- What time of day
- What day of the week
- How soon, etc.

Having a show should make sense to you. The members of your team are very important to the infrastructure of your brand. Everyone should be on the same page regarding the vision and the mission of the show.

When selecting the **WHAT FOR**, discuss this with your team . . . take suggestions and ask questions. This allows your team members to feel involved and invested in the process. As this happens, you all share the responsibility to check the calendar for compatible dates and times that work for everyone. This way you are starting out <u>solid</u>. Now, understand that not everyone will always be pleased, and that *you are still the BOSS of this project* but at least most, if not all, will be considered in the initial planning. Finding a solid team is not easy. Folks always say they want to participate completely (invest time and self) until the real work has to be done. That's when the egos show up. A good boss delegates duties while still accomplishing major tasks. Of course, there are times when team members feel like they are working harder than you even though they aren't paying for anything or providing any necessary resources, their time is still of value and we must respect that. At the onset, let them know what the costs are for putting on this masterpiece, let them know that if they are not a brand partner then they aren't required to shell out any cash (which means *you are the bank <u>and</u> the check writer* and this makes *you the Boss*. The Boss is always working, and if we all work together then at the end of this process this can be a true win-win for everyone! Helping the team to feel needed and an integral part of the process is the way to brand and keep them happy while building your brand.

Your Guide to a Perfect Fashion Show Production

Your Venue

One of your most challenging decisions will be the place you hold your event . . . your venue. So many things have to be considered, and this can truly stress your nerves--but don't let it. For example, let's look at some real challenges you are going to face as you search.

Is this place centrally located? WHY is this important? Because you don't want to take people too far out of their primary locations. For example, if you live in Midtown you wouldn't want to secure a venue out in Newman just because it cost you less money! Nine times out of ten, the complaint will be that it is too far! If you live in Midtown, most of the people you know and associate with are probably around five to twenty-five miles away unless they live out of town; so consider that when scouting!

Is there ample parking? There is nothing more frustrating than having a wonderful venue, your guests bought tickets, yet they are forced to walk up or down a steep hill, wade through some water, dodge undesirables, and ultimately forced to hail a taxi just to get to the front door of the venue and then, of course, do the same things after the event to get back to the car and discover they have to pay $20 to get their car out of the parking garage!!!! (Surely, I exaggerate, of course . . . but we've all been there . . . even for simpler excursions when we're in jeans and flats but for this event folks are all dressed and pressed and would truly prefer the venue have its own parking outside, yes?) SO PLEASE . . . Make sure there is ample parking for your staff and your guests AT YOUR VENUE'S LOCATION. As I eluded above . . . most ladies will probably be in heels, and walking too far will certainly not be welcomed!

Is there enough space for hair, makeup and models? Always remember the place you select must accommodate the project and its participants -- so don't cramp folks unnecessarily: think *space, space, space!!* I know this is something we all want to guarantee.

Does the place have adequate heat and/or air conditioning? To every extent possible, guaranteeing the comfort of your audience and participants is KEY. No air conditioning, no heat? No way!! Common sense dictates that if you have people crammed into a dressing room, which is sometimes unavoidable--whether it's four or forty-four people--and they are changing clothes, touching up hair and doing makeup for models that are running down a runway only to come back and do it again for eight scenes -- everyone will be HOT!!! I have seen photos of shows where folks are fanning themselves with napkins and dabbing their necks!! (Heads up! I keep an ol' slick fan situation because baby I can't handle too much heat in the event hall--that would cause me to leave. In fact, I once left a venue because of heat and seating. As a matter of fact . . .

About the seating. Okay, Great! You have a sold-out event! BUT PLEASE, PLEASE HAVE ADEQUATE SEATING, dolls! If you are renting a hall, be sure to ask up front if there is an available chair setup (and enough chairs to accommodate each body you expect to attend), and find out if the seating is included in the initial price. As a matter of fact, ALWAYS KNOW WHAT IS INCLUDED IN THE PRICE. One way to make this determination is to ask yourself what you would personally want available to you--that is, what would make you most comfortable if you were one of the attendees.

EXAMPLE

I know this might sound crazy, but I actually attended an event where the floors were solid concrete and there were maybe ten chairs available. This was a launch that started an hour late and ladies were standing on this concrete floor in heels, myself included! Girl! I was steamin! To support my colleagues, I tried to hold out and see what they had to offer, and when the first scene finally started and some foolishness came down the runway and those girls couldn't walk, for me it was done and done, finished and out!

The sound system. Yes. You will need a DJ; however, you have to make sure the hall, the bar, etc., will connect to speakers--or if they already have speakers at the venue--and that the speakers are able to distribute excellent sound wherever someone is sitting, standing or walking. There is nothing more disturbing than getting to the venue and learning that your DJ doesn't have everything s/he needs because you never checked to see if the venue was equipped to accommodate your DJ.

Restrooms. Yes, you heard me . . . restrooms!! CLEAN RESTROOMS are of the UTMOST IMPORTANCE! Your guests will blame ANY nastiness on you and your event, whether you own the venue or not. Be sure the owners already have someone to clean thoroughly for your event. For example, the party they hosted the night before has NOTHING to do with you or your event. You paid for a clean, walk-in, guest-ready venue. Make sure that's what you get.

When searching for a venue, REMEMBER that Saturdays will most likely be the most expensive day to rent the space, especially if it's a popular location with regular weekend night parties. Halls may pose this same challenge if they are in high demand. Fridays are also not so good for events because people who work all week usually don't get off until 5:00 pm . . . *then* there is the traffic . . . *then* they have to get home to change, take care of the household . . . *then* get out of the door to travel to your event. So many of these people won't bother or won't be able to attend. Consider this when selecting a venue because you do want a packed house, RIGHT?! Sundays are a nice day for this type of event, especially if you do a brunch time event. This is a more cost-effective day of the week for the venue as they usually don't have much going on for Sunday. Be sure to schedule it after church service and before 7:00 pm--those are prime times for Sunday. WHY? Because the work week is just a few hours away and folks like to get home to prepare.

Make sure the venue provides a reception area if you intend to sell tickets at the door or have a red carpet area. If your event happens during the winter months, be sure to ask about a coat check area. Now, <u>don't</u> go and get this huge venue that seats 1,000 people if you can't genuinely anticipate 1,000 people in attendance. If this is your first event, be smart about your selections. And it never hurts to ask somebody who knows if you're not sure.

Types of Venues

- Bars
- Halls
- Poolside
- Church
- Outdoor spaces
- Art Galleries
- Restaurants
- Mansions
- Yachts

Your Designers

Once you find your venue, decide what you want to showcase: clothing, jewelry, shoes, handbags, glasses . . . whether you want to have a winter, spring, summer or fall theme . . . and the color scheme, etc. This way you can select designers accordingly and lock them in. Get your designers involved in the casting process; they could have a preferred list of models or signature models which would make the casting much easier. Designers are also great to have for the actual casting because they can see who works well with their garments. Trust and believe this will help cut down all of the backstage drama that happens at EVERY show. You will be better equipped to handle whatever comes your way!

Have a *Strong Opener* and a *Strong (anticipated) Closer!* I know we all want to please our friends, but if your friend isn't the best designer then the opening or closing position is not for your friend. Don't make your friend your number one stunner for the night. It could ruin your event!

PLEASE DO NOT have twenty-two designers in one show. At best have eight--four at the top of the show, then intermission, and then bring the FIYA for the four in your second half. Start strong and finish stronger! Each designer should be responsible for an eight- to ten-piece collection that tells a story and is cohesive. Some folks want to show twenty pieces on the runway. No! You don't want your guests yawning in their seats or leaving in the middle of the show. There is nothing tackier or more disappointing than having a packed house before intermission and returning to a slew of empty seats.

If you should choose to charge a designer, PLEASE be sure to have something to offer them. *For example:* media coverage from bloggers, magazines, professional photos, personal brand interviews, buyers from boutiques in the audience, exclusive website coverage for a limited time, etc. Think this through: you cannot have a show without designers or models--these two elements are crucial unless you want to have a hot mess like the infamous *"She by You-Know-Who"* 😏 non-fashion show. Be mindful that the designers are buying fabrics and exerting lots of manpower, (sweat equity, if you will) while creating this collection for YOUR show.

I have accompanied a few designers and really watched them in action—I mean truly watched them sketch, create patterns, purchase fabric, cut out fabric, and go back and forth on what results they want for hours on end and then sew a complete collection after long hours of working at their full-time jobs only to come home and work some more to ready themselves for an event—and then on top of all that . . . once at the event make adjustments to the garments. I have seen them bring sewing machines to their hotel rooms and dressing rooms in order to accommodate EVERYONE involved. Understanding their process is the first step to appreciating the time they invest to help make YOUR SHOW the very best it can be. I get that you are providing a platform, but please remember that in addition to working all of those hours at home and on site while simultaneously holding down daily jobs, these designers are making a financial investment as well.

Review Points

- Email the designers and have a group meeting about your show
- Get designers involved in the casting process
- Allow designers to use their signature models
- Do not have a million designers in one show
- Have a Strong Opener and Strong Closer for your show

MsNickee Mack

Models ... Casting Call ...Casting Call Location

Models and casting calls go hand in hand! Between you and your team you should have a strong network of models to send emails, inbox messages, and text messages to in order to get the word out. I also suggest engaging with social media and joining model and designer groups in order to create a buzz! Get your verbiage together for model call flyers. You should already know **WHY, WHAT FOR, and WHEN**. You can also do an online call for those models who are located out of town. Create an email address just for the call so that no emails go unnoticed! When doing an online model call you should require a headshot, a full body shot, stats (height, waist, bust and hips), and video footage of the model's runway walk.

When conducting a physical casting, require that all models dress in either all black or white and denim. This is crucial. WHY? ... Because those that don't pay attention and show up looking any ol' way they please are the ones you will have problems with later on during your production process when it comes to following your instructions. LISTENING and <u>following instructions</u> are first, second and foremost in having a successful production. EVERYONE should have specific instructions for which they are held accountable.

All online submissions have a <u>deadline</u> and a model registration for those physically attending the model call. Designers who have signature models should have already provided the required documentation for all model participation in the show; this allows you to know exactly how many models you will need.

DO NOT CHARGE MODELS TO COME TO A MODEL CALL. WHY? First, you cannot have a fashion show without models or designers. Second, models that are selected give of their time for rehearsals, meetings, and/or on the day of the show they will literally be there all day to bring <u>your</u> vision to life. Third, you will not get the quality models that have a following by charging them to participate.

IMPORTANT ~ **Adopt a standard.** We all have one or even a few friends that feel like they should model, e.g., a model's mom who feels like she should still model; the clerk at the corner store who used to model back in the 90's and appeared in a throwback video who believes she can still rock the runway. DON'T DO IT! Models who don't have the look or the walk or the size to compliment the garments should not be on the runway, PERIOD! Runway models invest in their own success.

GET THIS! THE ABILITY TO WALK IS A MUST! I know some of the most *unattractive* models who are absolute beasts on the runway, and I would book them in a heartbeat because

Your Guide to a Perfect Fashion Show Production

they can sell wool to a sheep. By the way, they *perform* on the runway! Walking is Key!

One last message on this topic:

TO THE MODELS: PICTURES ARE IMPORTANT!! Your comp card should be professional and should contain your headshot and maybe two to three professional diverse shots of you . . . not pictures of you on the runway and not pictures of you at the club because you were cute . . . not pixilated shots of you taken from your cell phone . . . not your best friend's wedding picture cut in half. Now, can you print your own? Sure! It's more cost-effective; but make sure it's a photo printer or go to a facility that prints photos perfectly on photo card stock! PRESENT GREAT PHOTOS. That's all the recipient will have to remember you by when you leave the casting!

Your casting call location should be spacious enough for your models to actually get the feel of walking on a runway. The casting call should be an in-and-out process: Get them registered, give them a number, have them walk and then *Thank you!* Decide who you really want for the show after the initial call. You don't want to take up a lot of time in the space as you will probably have a cut-off time, and you don't want to exceed that time . . . you're paying for it! You will need time after the call for a group discussion with the panel of judges. Make sure the judges that you choose are experienced in runway walks or simply use your designers as judges; they know what they want to see on the runway when models are in their garments! Do not use friends who have nothing to do with the show process, you open the door for small talk, laughs and giggles instead of a PROFESSIONAL CASTING atmosphere!

Review Points

- Require models to have a headshot and full body shots
- Create an email address for your production
- Conduct online casting for out of town models
- DO NOT CHARGE models for model call
- Have a professional Comp Card
- Have a standard

The Host

There's the host who likes to stand and read from a cue card, the host who creates excitement, and the host who barely speaks. Whichever your preference, start looking immediately! You should send out official company emails to desired hosts to grab their attention, and **PLEASE BE READY TO PAY.** I am not talking about a small fortune, but these people have to stand up and be "ON" all night entertaining your audience. Respect their time and don't insult them by asking them to do it for free. Most hosts do this for a living. It's their regular job/income #IJS!!!

A good host helps sell throughout the show by mentioning brands, and you can require them to do so. Provide a typed list of your designers, special mentions, guests, scene order and designer's names so they can go over all of this before the show!

Perhaps you're asking: *How do I acquire a host?* Well, expect to place a deposit with the host or their management in order to be placed on their calendar. When the host arrives, it is customary to provide a separate dressing area and pay them upon arrival. This is a great business move because word of mouth is a very powerful media tool. In fact, it's considered the absolute best tried and true media tool. A great host speaks to many people, so think of it as a marketing move.

Review Points

- Remember to do your homework on knowing the style of the host you choose.
- Have an official letter when requesting a host.
- Make sure when you have secured your host they have correct show info.
- Prepare to pay for a host in advance to secure them.
- Be sure to have a host that is used to getting your crowd's attention

Allow me to speak on this particular picture above. The venue had no mics and the place was packed. Fortunately for them, the host knew how to engage with the audience, had a voice that carried,

made it her business to be in the center of the room to address the audience, and yes . . . you guessed it . . . I was that host! Experienced hosts can make a way out of no way!

THE MAKEUP ARTIST AND HAIR STYLIST

Now, here's when you can call on all of those folks you already have a great relationship with because you will need leads in both of these areas that your team can go to when and if an issue arises. You should not have to address styling issues on the day of the show.

This is what you will do . . .

Contact beauty schools in your local area at least a month or so in advance of your show (no later) and get the students to come out; some of them are really good. Offer to come to the school to see their work and offer class credits, gift bags . . . something to encourage them to provide their services.

Team leads should be paid because . . .

They will be the ones handling the hustle and bustle in that arena, and more often than not it gets really chaotic. Paying them gives them the incentive they need to be prepared and effective! Team leads should be seasoned individuals with experience working backstage at fashion shows; they will be quick on faces and understand the hustle and flow. Now, I know we like to hire friends or allow friends that can beat their own faces to work in shows, but just because they can do their own face doesn't mean they can do someone else's. Ask to see their work on someone else's face. Your artist should be able to do all skin colors and types, and it would help if you have a look *you prefer* for hair and makeup. You must specify that the teams are not applying FULL HEADS OF WEAVE and hair. Be sure to tell the team to bring complete kits. Also, speak with your leads about desired face and makeup looks so that all of your models will look consistent on the runway!

Cold-call the school . . .

Find out if the school has any interest in having its students participate in a major show for class credits. When contacting schools be sure to secure the name and contact information for the school's DIRECTOR. Visit the school and get to know the teachers of the programs you are interested in working with, introduce them to your brand, have your social media info for them, and help them get excited about what you are planning! Prepare a formal proposal for them.

Review Points

- Secure leads in both hair and makeup areas.
- Contact beauty schools in your area at least a month out from your event.
- Be prepared to pay team leads.
- Be sure to have a *look* already selected for the team.

YOUR DJ

Music is a requirement! People relate to music. Music builds excitement. It allows your audience to readily engage with what's happening on the runway. You want a DJ who is up to date with all the latest music, who knows how to entertain a crowd with music. The designers can either provide their own music or you can provide the DJ with something to play that complements the scene. Ideally, the music should be discussed and received early on in the planning stages. As soon as you select your DJ, the designers should be notified and given his/her email address and/or phone number so that if they have specific songs they prefer, these songs can be emailed to him/her and placed on a playlist. As producer of the show, you should have a lineup of designers in order . . . having them in order will help the DJ to prepare the music according to each scene. I can't tell you how many times this directive has not been followed and a song designated for a particular designer was played before its time. Designers HATE that! Another key factor is to tell your DJ up front that you will need a cordless mic for your host!

Videography/Photography

It's always wonderful to have pictures and footage of your event. It would be wise to discuss what your videographer and/or photographic needs are <u>before</u> the event. There have been shows when we did not receive the footage! An *advance discussion and contractual agreement* between you and the professionals explaining that NOTHING should be posted or leaked until you have the original copies is required. You need to see EVERYTHING! Have a specific area for them to be placed, discuss the layout of the show so they know when and where the models are coming out so that you can be sure to have some great promo footage for your next event. Have a dedicated photographer for the red carpet--one that can secure pictures <u>and</u> interviews! Also you should have a step and repeat (backdrop with sponsors and your own logo all over it) for your guests to take pictures in front of. Secure dedicated photography time for this location. You should order this step and repeat backdrop as soon as you know who your sponsors are!

The following sites have always worked wonders for me:

- www.stepandrepeatla.com
- www.stickersbanners.net
- www.sign11.com/step-and-repeat

Review Points

- Have a contract between you and videographer/photographer
- Review all footage before released to the public
- Have a dedicated photographer for special areas

Entertainment

This can be whatever you want it to be: poets, singers, dedications, dancers, comedians . . . the sky's the limit in this area. Keep it short and sweet to avoid boring your guests. Remember, your guests came to see FASHION. Although it serves as a great intermediary, the entertainment should be treated just that way . . . as an intermediary. Make sure it's truly entertaining . . . NOT your best friend's cousin's uncle who lives downstairs and sings in the shower or the choir director's sister's organist that dances on the side but sings background for a cover band . . . NONE of that! Don't book anyone without an audition. See your "talent" way before you book it/them. If you decide to have a feature talent, this should be someone with a huge following and someone you would more than likely have to pay for! And remember . . . *you get what you pay for* . . . so the easiest way to save money would be to do a Dedication [What is this?] This is when you have a cause or charity event connected to your show. Someone speaks on the issue of the cause/charity. You could give an award of appreciation to those helping with that cause/charity and have them share a testimonial! Make this short and sweet!

Review Points

- HEAR and SEE the talents' TALENT
- Pay for feature talent
- For dedications, have people with great testimonies!

Backstage Manager Front-of-House Ticketmaster Front-of-House Floor Manager

These are the people you trust the most and who will comprise your TEAM. Basically, they are responsible for double-checking and guaranteeing all of the aforementioned items have been satisfied.

More specifically, they ...

- help with the flow of the show
- take the money at the door
- tell you if something is awry on the runway
- make sure the seating is right
- guide your VIP guests
- prepare special gift bags and distribute them accordingly
- keep you calm when they see you becoming overwhelmed, because this WILL HAPPEN
- make small issues go away

They comprise the team that's with you when the show is over.

This is the team you should be working with from the start of your production.

They should be aware of everything that's happening with the show. This will ensure that you all stay on the same page.

Remember, YOU ARE THE BOSS. You make the final decisions, but they are your liaisons for what you can't see or might have missed! You <u>must</u> communicate with your team regularly to be certain they are aware of your needs and preferences for your event. You can't be everywhere at once, so make sure you and your team are communicating effectively on the day of the event.

Review Points

- The people who form your team are those you TRUST the most
- This team shares your vision and mission
- This team has the run of the show printed out

RUNWAY SETUP

Whether you are building a stage or utilizing an existing stage, your Front-of-House Manager (FHM) must be aware of the runway setup for the floor. These areas should remain clear at all times for entry and exit of the models.

If you should have a packed house, having a floor setup is extremely important. As previously indicated, you will need dedicated space for your photographer and videographer to guarantee they can get great shots. Be sure to have all of the models walk this space.

Your Guide to a Perfect Fashion Show Production

Be mindful . . . You don't want any surprises like loose carpet, holes in the floor, slippery floors, etc. Your FHM will be responsible for this.

Decide immediately if you want to build a stage or use existing space. This is crucial to the flow of the show. If you are using portable or stationary stairs, PLEASE have someone at the foot of the stairs to assist the models up and down. Oftentimes, portable steps are not as sturdy as we would like to think they are. Make sure whatever setup you choose is audience-friendly so that no sections prevent your audience from seeing the items coming down the runway!

Review Points

- Have dedicated area for your models and photographer
- Make sure your FHM knows the flow of the show and floor plan
- DO a COMPLETE RUN/REHEARSAL of the show before the actual event
- Use assistants when using portable or stationary stairs
- Have runway setup options such as the following . . .

MsNickee Mack

Your Guide to a Perfect Fashion Show Production

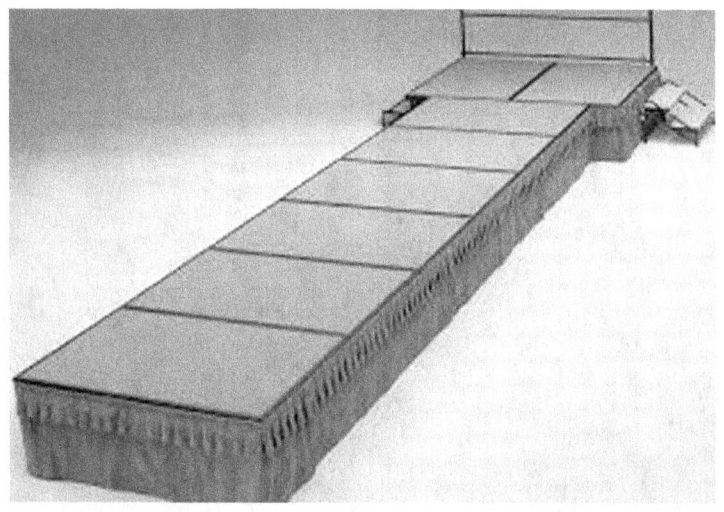

DRESSING ROOM SETUP

You should have a large enough space for all models, hair and makeup, and designers! Do not short-change yourself with this: YOU DO NOT WANT A SITUATION WITHOUT ENOUGH ROOM/SPACE . . . this makes for unhappy models, designers and stylists! Word of mouth is everything. When your backstage people are unhappy THEY TALK, and this could have a negative impact on how well your future shows are viewed. Remember, SPACE, SPACE, SPACE! If you don't think you yourself would be comfortable in the area, then neither will they! Take everyone into consideration and REMEMBER . . . WORD OF MOUTH is everything and having a great backstage production where the dressing room flows on point is crucial.

For example, your hair and makeup should NOT BE near the designers. Your ideal setup would be to have your hair, makeup and models all in one space so that when the models come in they can sign up and wait for their service(s) to be performed.

Always specify that models should...

- Arrive with clean hair and face and have lashes on or bring a pair with them
- Have clean hair
- NOT receive a full weave
- If at all possible, display the preferred looks for your show (this will eliminate any confusion)

Review Points

- Be sure to have enough space for hair and makeup
- Require models to be clean and bring their own lashes
- Make sure you have a room where there are plenty of outlets or buy strips/extensions
- See dressing room setup options below...

Your Guide to a Perfect Fashion Show Production

VENDORS/SPONSORS

A way to build a good network is by collaborating with other brands. This will benefit your production financially. We all know friends and family that have special skills and talents, but those with tangible products can become vendors at your event and help build their brand recognition. How can you do this? Talk to friends and family, go on social media and join vendors groups, go to your local stores . . . e.g., mom and pop joints that know you--tell them about your show and see if they would like to vend or sponsor Note: It would be great to have a cause behind your show when approaching people for sponsorship. Donors consider it worthy to be affiliated with causes that help the community. Online boutiques that are local for jewelry, handbags, shoes, candles, and gift baskets are also good contacts. Approach larger brands with a professional presentation if you find you have the same target market; sometimes they will see your vision, sponsor you, and build a lasting relationship. When you have secured the vendors, be sure to dedicate a space for them. Having vendors at the entrance of the event space is always a good look. That allows them to be the first thing guests see when entering the building. Your vendors have paid to be a part of your event, so show your respect for their business and their products by placing them front and center, if at all possible, and during your intermission have your host shout out these vendors and do a brief Flash Sale . . . something special like *"Special pricing for the next 15 minutes!"* This could possibly make the difference in whether or not a vendor sells anything at your event.

Your Guide to a Perfect Fashion Show Production

Review Points

- Secure your vendors early
- Have a reasonable vendor package set up for smaller brands
- Have a professional proposal for larger brands

MEDIA

Secure some type of media for your event, e.g., magazines, bloggers, TV, web shows, red carpet hosts with web shows, radio shows, etc. If they have a radio show, ask to be on the show to talk about your upcoming event! Most of these entities are building their brands and would love to build a broader audience. So, if approached properly they may even help promote your event as long as the event promotes them. Let them know their logo will go on all social media, backdrops, and promotional items like flyers and banners. Online media outlets are great to partner with as they already have followers that are usually looking for great events to attend, and if you partner with them that's great free promotion. You can also use online radio hosts to man your red carpet area, because they are already accustomed to interviewing people and again they have a following and might offer live streaming.

Review Points

- Contact media in advance
- Offer pre-advertisement with their logo
- Get on their show!

You Have to Pay to Play

When it's time to pay people for their services be sure to have a contract already in place for each. Some will differ from others; some require a deposit with final payment upon arrival--this is customary for Hosts. With some services, you can arrange to pay at the end of the night. My advice is pay as many people up front as you can . . . having initially secured the contract that states if services are not rendered as contracted, you will take legal action. *This is not personal. It's business.* Steer clear of sentiment. They owe you the deposit. Compassion and understanding are expected. For instance, you might give them a second chance, but they must still be held accountable for the terms of the contract, which is where the reimbursement applies. A second chance might be that you both agree to their providing their services at your very next event *free of charge* to satisfy the terms of the contract and if not, they will be responsible for the entire amount due.

EXAMPLE

You pay someone up front and on the day of the show, they don't show up due to a family emergency, etc. Yes, be understanding; however, please know that they now owe you money because you paid a deposit. Trust and believe if they provide a service for your event and you don't pay them that would never work. Were the situation reversed, you could probably depend on them smearing your name, your brand and suing you. I learned a valuable lesson with an event I did in Florida two years in a row with agreement of payment. I was sentimental about it, giving the benefit of the doubt and I got royally burned. LESSON LEARNED. Use my experience for YOUR LESSON!

Just So You Know

Producing a show can be fun, but it can also be stressful. Following these steps I have provided will ensure that you won't miss anything and as your brand grows, you will learn to handle its growth. Having a plan will also help the people who choose to participate in your core team to realize that you are serious. There's nothing like putting together something that comes from the heart. It's invigorating! You can see your own growth, it makes you proud, so be PREPARED for anything. Have a Plan B just in case crazy situations arise, because they will. Don't get flustered . . . stay the course . . . get it done!

Are you wondering if you should sell advance tickets? Of course! Promote! Promote! Promote! Social Media is a great way to promote; be sure to connect all of your social media outlets together like Facebook to Twitter, to Instagram, to tumblr . . . you know what I mean . . . and post often! If you have certain people that you have already secured for the show . . . e.g., models, hosts, entertainers . . . post their photos together with your brand logo and theirs to create a buzz. Get the show flyer to them ASAP so that they too can post the flyer as often as possible.

Your Guide to a Perfect Fashion Show Production

I'm going to say something that might not set well with a few of you but the TRUTH hurts sometime. If you have to charge the models to audition, then you don't have a budget for the show. WHY am I against this? Well, ask yourself this: If a model comes to audition and at the door you have sign-up and registration and you charge $5 to $25 at this time, then they hit the runway and they are terrible . . . no one judging likes anything they are doing on the runway and at the end of the casting you have about 30 people that you know will not be in your show. Do you return their money? Most of the time . . . wait let me tell the truth . . . ALL of the time that's a NO, and honestly "that's not fair." If they don't make the cut then give them their money back, because you are padding your pocket and counting on that dollar and cent to build your budget. Not good.

You also get those that charge and select everyone who comes to audition whether they are good or awful and that shows you have no "standard." You're just seeing it from a perspective of "if I have 100 models and each one invites one person, I will at least have a decent crowd. No! Don't count on them to build your crowd. That is <u>your</u> job!

I have also encountered people who have given up in the middle of planning a production and that just shoots your credibility straight to the depths. Was the money returned? NO! No one will trust you to finish anything. You have wasted people's time and damaged your brand reputation before you even got anything off the ground.

I also want you to consider this: sometimes the designers create an entire collection for a themed show and unfortunately they may sell nothing. Models spend all day at your event and get no significant networking and no pay, yet they had a great time. Post and share these pictures and create a following for your next event. They rock hard for your brand! Now, does it still sound fair to charge them?

I have worked with some amazing people in this industry, and I want to share with you a few words from some of the amazing talent that I have had the pleasure of producing projects for, trained in modeling, helped brand their brands, and more:

Telethia Penn Professional National and International Model and Celebrity Hair stylist

Ok I've been thinking of quotes when it comes to you and your work ethic in general. I keep coming back to one in particular "never let 'em see you sweat." We both know that behind the scenes of a show is crazy but when you come out as a model or production head you are chill and everything works and looks like a well-oiled machine I Love that about you. Another one I like that I think describes you is "The difference between ordinary and extraordinary is that little extra" . . . you always put a little extra on anything you do to make it great.

Your Guide to a Perfect Fashion Show Production

Temeka Ramsey
a/k/a Professional Designer of "Diva By Temeka"

MsNickee Mack "one word no period" is the epitome of Passion, Professionalism, and Poise. I have had the opportunity to work with her while participating in runway shows and she exudes the passion required to survive in this industry. She always wants the best for all involved . . . . The designer, the models, and those holding the reigns of producing a show. Her professionalism is one that is direct and to the point but it gets the business in order. When placed into a position out of her realm of responsibility, I have seen her get into action and produce a show seamlessly; you would have never known she acquired the responsibility 4 hours prior to the event's start time. Yaaassssss darling.....need a show produced? Need the baddest walking models for your event or shoot? Need to make solid connections in the industry??? Then call "MsNickee" . . . one word no period.

Alexandria Robinson Owner of Born Thik/Professional Plus Model and Featured on Love and Hip Hop Atlanta

To know her is to love her. It has been my honor and pleasure to know MsNickee. She has been a friend, a confidant, and now my manager. Before signing to Diva Day International, I was a freelance curvy model. I've done work with other organizations and something just didn't feel right.

I came to MsNickee a couple of years ago with an idea for a brand for myself. We were talking and riding and she explained some things to me and the one thing that she has NEVER done, was put me or my ideas down. She has always been supportive. Truth be told, I tend to fumble my ideas together and need help focusing on one thing at a time, and she has helped me to do that. My brand is Born Thik and she helped me bring that to life with an Amazing production!

Since I became a sister in the Diva Day family, I have gained more confidence than I've ever had. My Diva Dolls support one another, and we are all there for the woman who brought us together. WHY?? Because she saw, and sees things in us even when we don't see it. MsNickee believes in our brands just as much as she does her own. She's very thorough and well calculated. And though she can be a very tough mentor, she does it out of love for her craft and her girls. MsNickee became the big sister I needed in my life to get through many trials. For that I am forever grateful to have her in my life. Diva Day Dolls stick together!

Every step of every event, good or bad, that happens in your life is exact! When you learn to live that truth, life becomes simple!

The review...

When I first heard MsNickee Mack's voice at a fashion show, I knew then that our lives were connected. The bigger than life personality was an absolute overwhelm but the bigger than life heart, I grew to know, was the absolute!!

MARCO MAYS

Co-Founder and the Image & Events Manager of InUR Image, a lifestyle management company specializing in Image and Brand Management. Front End Operations and Hospitality Coordinator of Full Figured Fashion Week and Ms. Full Figured HBCU Pageant

Resources

Keeping your brand safe:

Here is some trademark information . . .

Search the U.S. Patent and Trademark Office database to make sure that the trademark for your band's name doesn't already belong to somebody else. You can search the entire database online using the U.S. Patent and Trademark Office's Trademark Electronic Search System, or TESS.

http://www.uspto.gov/trademarks-getting-started/trademark-basics

There are sites that allow you to trademark your brand name as low as $69

Like: www.trademarkplus.com

www.sharpfilings.com/Trademarks

www.legalzoom.com/Trademarks

Here are some searches related to trademarking a brand name:

- how to patent a band name
- how to trademark my brand name
- how to find out if a BRAND name is trademarked

- trademarking a brand name
- trademark brand name class
- trademark brand name cost
- how to trademark a band name for free
- how much does it cost to trademark

PUT THESE IN YOUR GOOGLE SEARCH AND RESEARCH AS MUCH AS YOU CAN!

How to get sponsorship for a show:

Here are some links that may help you with that.

http://www.fashionindustrynetwork.com/forum/topics/how-to-get-sponsorship-for

http://www.ehow.com/how_6047803_fashion-show-sponsors.html

http://smallbusiness.chron.com/corpate-sponsors-event-25432.html

https://fashionmarketinglessons.wordpress.com/2010/12/15/how-to-find-a-sponsor-get-sponsorship-for-your-fashion-show-2/

In order to get a makeup and hair team together for your production you need to have resources. I have listed almost every cosmetology school in the country for you. All you have to do now is copy, past and Google.

When contacting the schools have your steps in order. See the chapter titled **The Makeup Artist and Hair Stylist.**

Your Guide to a Perfect Fashion Show Production

ATLANTA

Aveda Institute Atlanta - Atlanta, GA

Empire Beauty School - Atlanta-Northlake |Atlanta, GA

Empire Beauty School - Augusta, Augusta, GA

Empire Beauty School with campuses in . . .
- Atlanta-Dunwoody
- Atlanta-Kennesaw
- Atlanta-Lawrenceville
- Atlanta-Morrow
- Savannah

Georgia Career Institute (GA) - Conyers, GA

International School of Skin, Nailcare & Massage Therapy - Atlanta, GA

Miller-Motte Technical College - Augusta, GA

Miller-Motte Technical College - Macon, Macon, GA

Paul Mitchell the School Esani - Alpharetta, GA

The Keune Academy by 124 - Lawrenceville, GA

The Keune Academy by 124 - Atlanta, GA

Virginia College with campuses in . . .
- Augusta

- Columbus
- Macon
- Savannah

FLORIDA

American Institute - Margate, FL

Aveda Institute with campuses in . . .

- Clearwater
- Davie
- Jacksonville
- Tallahassee
- Winter Park

Beauty Schools of America *with campuses in* . . .

- Hialeah
- Homestead
- Miami
- North Miami Beach
- South Beach

Boca Beauty Academy - Boca Raton, FL

Cozmo Beauty School - Bonita Springs, FL

Daytona College - Ormond Beach, FL

Empire Beauty School - Fort Lauderdale, Lauderhill, FL

Empire Beauty School Lakeland-Winter Haven - Lakeland, FL

Empire Beauty School Tampa-Brandon - Tampa, FL

Empire Beauty School West Palm Beach - West Palm Beach, FL

Florida Academy - Fort Myers, FL

Florida Career College with campuses in . . .

- Boynton Beach
- Hialeah
- Jacksonville
- Kendall
- Kissimmee
- Lauderdale Lakes
- Margate
- Miami
- Orlando
- Pembroke Pines
- Tampa
- West Palm Beach

Fortis Institute - Pensacola, FL

Hair Benders Academy - Longwood, FL

Hollywood Institute of Beauty Careers with campuses in

- Miami Beach
- Orlando

- West Palm Beach

International Academy – South Daytona, FL

International Hair and Barber Academy - Boca Raton, FL

Loraine's Academy, Inc. – St. Petersburg, FL

Meridian College - Sarasota, FL

Palm Beach Academy of Health & Beauty - Lake Park, FL

Regency Beauty Institute *with campuses* in

- Carrollwood
- Fort Myers
- Jacksonville
- Orange Park

Sunstate Academy, Fort Myers, FL

TENAJ Salon Institute - The Villages, FL

The Hair Design Institute - Boynton Beach, FL

Virginia College - Jacksonville, FL

Virginia College - Pensacola, FL

Virginia College - Fort Pierce, FL

NEW YORK

Academy of NYC - Paul Mitchell Partner School – Staten Island

Your Guide to a Perfect Fashion Show Production

American Beauty School, Inc. – New York City

Aveda Institute – New York City

Capri Cosmetology Learning Center – Nanuet, NY

Capri Cosmetology Learning Center – Newburg, NY

Continental School of Beauty – Syracuse, NY

Empire Beauty School – Brooklyn, NY

Empire Beauty School – Buffalo, NY

Empire Beauty School – Westchester County – Peekskill, NY

Empire Beauty School – Rochester, NY

Empire Beauty Schools – New York City

Empire Beauty Schools – Queens, NY

Long Island Beauty School – Hempstead, NY

The Hair Design Institute – an affiliate of Long Island Beauty School

The Salon Professional Academy – South Plainfield, NJ and Tonawanda, NY

Westchester School of Beauty Culture – Mt. Vernon, NY

CALIFORNIA

Academy for Salon Professionals – Canoga Park, CA

Nickee Mack

Academy of Makeup & Fashion - Canoga Park, CA

Adrian' Beauty College of Tracy, Inc. - Tracy, CA

Adrian's Beauty College of Turlock - Turlock, CA

Alameda Beauty College - Alameda, CA

Aveda Institute Los Angeles - Los Angeles, CA

Bellus Academy East San Diego County Campus - El Cajon, CA

Bellus Academy North San Diego County Campus Poway, CA

Bellus Academy South San Diego County Campus National City, CA

Blake Austin College Vacaville, CA

Career Academy of Beauty Garden Grove, CA

Cinta Aveda Institute San Francisco, CA

COBA Academy Anaheim Metro Orange, CA

Dublin Beauty College Dublin, CA

Elite Cosmetology School Yucca Valley, CA

Federico Beauty Institute Sacramento, CA

Fremont Beauty College Fremont, CA

Hollywood Beauty College Stockton, CA

Your Guide to a Perfect Fashion Show Production

Lu Ross Academy of Beauty & Health Ventura, CA

Marinello Schools of Beauty Anaheim, CA

Marinello Schools of Beauty Bakersfield, CA

Marinello Schools of Beauty Bell, CA

Marinello Schools of Beauty Burbank, CA

Marinello Schools of Beauty Castro Valley, CA

Marinello Schools of Beauty Cathedral City, CA

Marinello Schools of Beauty Chico, CA

Marinello Schools of Beauty City of Industry, CA

Marinello Schools of Beauty Concord, CA

Marinello Schools of Beauty El Cajon, CA

Marinello Schools of Beauty Fresno, CA

Marinello Schools of Beauty Hayward, CA

Marinello Schools of Beauty Hemet, CA

Marinello Schools of Beauty Huntington Beach, CA

Marinello Schools of Beauty Inglewood, CA

Marinello Schools of Beauty Lake Forest, CA

Marinello Schools of Beauty Lomita, CA

Marinello Schools of Beauty Los Angeles East, CA

Marinello Schools of Beauty Los Angeles West, CA

Marinello Schools of Beauty Moreno Valley, CA

Marinello Schools of Beauty Murrieta, CA

Marinello Schools of Beauty Napa, CA

Marinello Schools of Beauty Ontario, CA

Marinello Schools of Beauty Palmdale, CA

Marinello Schools of Beauty Paramount, CA

Marinello Schools of Beauty Redding, CA

Marinello Schools of Beauty Reseda, CA

Marinello Schools of Beauty Sacramento, CA

Marinello Schools of Beauty San Bernardino, CA

Marinello Schools of Beauty San Diego Miramar, CA

Marinello Schools of Beauty San Francisco, CA

Marinello Schools of Beauty San Mateo, CA

Marinello Schools of Beauty San Rafael, CA

Marinello Schools of Beauty Santa Clara, CA

Marinello Schools of Beauty Seaside, CA

Your Guide to a Perfect Fashion Show Production

Marinello Schools of Beauty Simi Valley, CA

Marinello Schools of Beauty Stockton, CA

Marinello Schools of Beauty Victorville, CA

Marinello Schools of Beauty Visalia, CA

Marinello Schools of Beauty West Covina, CA

Marinello Schools of Beauty Whittier, CA

Milan Institute Bakersfield, CA

Milan Institute Clovis / Fresno area, CA

Milan Institute of Cosmetology Fairfield, CA

Milan Institute of Cosmetology La Quinta, CA

Milan Institute of Cosmetology Visalia, CA

Modern Beauty Academy Oxnard, CA

Napoleon Perdis Makeup Academy Hollywood, CA

Newberry School of Beauty Granada Hills, CA

North Adrian's Beauty College Modesto, CA

Palace Beauty College Los Angeles, CA

Royale College of Beauty Temecula, CA

Ruby Makeup Academy North Hollywood, CA

Ruby Makeup Academy San Gabriel Valley, CA

Ruby Makeup Academy Upland, CA

Safavi Institute of Cosmetology and Esthetics, a Paul Mitchell Partner School Modesto, CA

Salon Success Academy Corona, CA

Salon Success Academy Fontana, CA

Salon Success Academy Redlands, CA

Salon Success Academy San Bernardino, CA

Salon Success Academy Upland, CA

The American Institute of Education (A.I.E.) Santa Ana, CA

TONI&GUY Academy Costa Mesa, CA

Toni&Guy Academy Santa Monica, CA

W Institute of Cosmetology, Concord, CA

Western Beauty Institute, Fullerton, CA

Western Beauty Institute, Lancaster, CA

Western Beauty Institute, Panorama City, CA

ARIZONA

Academy of Advanced Aesthetics & Permanent Cosmetics Peoria, AZ

Your Guide to a Perfect Fashion Show Production

Academy of Advanced Aesthetics & Permanent Cosmetics Scottsdale, AZ

Academy of Nail Technology Phoenix, AZ

Avalon School of Cosmetology Mesa, AZ

Avalon School of Cosmetology Phoenix, AZ

Aveda Institute Phoenix Tempe, AZ

Aveda Institute Tucson Tucson, AZ

Brillare Hairdressing Academy Phoenix Chandler, AZ

Brillare Hairdressing Academy Scottsdale, AZ

Carsten Institute of Cosmetology Tempe, AZ

Eastern Arizona Academy of Cosmetology Safford, AZ

Empire Beauty School Avondale Goodyear Avondale Goodyear, AZ

Empire Beauty School Chandler Gilbert Chandler Gilbert, AZ

Empire Beauty School Flagstaff Flagstaff, AZ

Empire Beauty School North Tucson Mall Area North Tucson Mall Area, AZ

Empire Beauty School Phoenix Glendale Phoenix Glendale, AZ

Empire Beauty School Phoenix Paradise Valley Phoenix Paradise Valley , AZ

Empire Beauty School Prescott Prescott, AZ

Empire Beauty School Tucson University Area Tucson University Area, AZ

G Skin and Beauty Institute Arizona Chandler, AZ

IMAj Institute Scottsdale, AZ

International Academy of Beauty Desert Sky Phoenix, AZ

International Academy of Beauty Mesa, AZ

International Academy of Beauty Metro Center Phoenix, AZ

International Academy of Beauty Tempe, AZ

Nail Logic The Institute of Nail Technology Mesa, AZ

National Laser Institute Scottsdale, AZ

Penrose Academy, formerly Kohler Academy Scottsdale, AZ

Regency Beauty Institute East Tucson Tucson East, AZ

Regency Beauty Institute Mesa Mesa, AZ

Regency Beauty Institute Metro Center Phoenix, AZ

Regency Beauty Institute North Tucson Tucson North, AZ

Regency Beauty Institute Tolleson Phoenix / Tolleson, AZ

Southwest Institute of Natural Aesthetics Tempe, AZ

Steiner Institute of Esthetics Phoenix Phoenix, AZ

Steiner Institute of Esthetics Tempe Tempe, AZ

Studio Academy of Beauty Chandler, AZ

Studio Academy of Beauty Phoenix, AZ

The Skin & Makeup Institute of Arizona Peoria, AZ

Toni & Guy Academy Scottsdale, AZ

ARKANSAS

Career Academy of Hair Design - Springdale, AR

imagine Paul Mitchell Partner School North Little Rock, AR

Regency Beauty Institute Fayetteville Fayetteville, AR

Regency Beauty Institute Little Rock Little Rock, AR

The Salon Professional Academy North Little Rock , AR

Washington Barber College Little Rock, AR

COLORADO

Aveda Institute Denver Denver, CO

College of International Esthetics, Inc. Arvada, CO

Empire Beauty School Arvada Westminster Wheat Ridge Arvada Wheat Ridge, CO

Empire Beauty School Aurora Denver Aurora Denver, CO

Empire Beauty School Lakewood West Denver Lakewood West Denver, CO

Empire Beauty School Littleton South Lakewood Littleton South Lakewood, CO

Empire Beauty School Thornton Denver Thornton Denver, CO

Heritage College Denver, CO

IntelliTec College Pueblo Pueblo , CO

International Salon and Spa Academy Colorado Springs, CO

Longs Peak Academy Longmont, CO

New Dimensions Beauty Academy Parker, CO

Regency Beauty Institute Ft. Collins Ft. Collins, CO

Regency Beauty Institute Lakewood Lakewood, CO

Regency Beauty Institute Westminster Westminster, CO

The Salon Professional Academy Colorado Springs, CO

The Salon Professional Academy Grand Junction, CO

Toni&Guy Hairdressing Colorado Springs, CO

Xenon International Academy Aurora, CO

CONNECTICUT

Academy Di Capelli Wallingford, CT

Branford Academy of Hair & Cosmetology Branford, CT

Marinello Schools of Beauty, formerly Brio Academy East Hartford, CT

Marinello Schools of Beauty, formerly Brio Academy Enfield, CT

Marinello Schools of Beauty, formerly Brio Academy Fairfield, CT

Marinello Schools of Beauty, formerly Brio Academy Hamden, CT

Marinello Schools of Beauty, formerly Brio Academy Meriden, CT

Marinello Schools of Beauty, formerly Brio Academy Niantic, CT

Marinello Schools of Beauty, formerly Brio Academy Torrington, CT

Marinello Schools of Beauty, formerly Brio Academy Willimantic, CT

Oxford Academy of Hair Design Seymour, CT

Ricci's Academy of Cosmetology Newtown, CT

Sono Academy Norwalk, CT

The European Academy of Cosmetology & Hairdressing Guilford, CT

Total Look Academy Southport, CT

DELAWARE

Academy of Massage & Bodywork Bear, DE

American Beauty Academy Wilmington, DE

Delaware Learning Institute of Cosmetology Dagsboro, DE

DISTRICT OF COLUMBIA

Aveda Institute Washington DC Washington, DC

HAWAII

IBS School of Cosmetology Kahului, HI

IDAHO

Idaho Permanent Makeup Eagle, ID

Milan Institute Nampa, ID

The Hair Academy Paul Mitchell Partner School Rexburg, ID

The School of Hairstyling Chubbuck, ID

TONI&GUY Hairdressing Academy Boise, ID

TONI&GUY Hairdressing Academy Coeur d'Alene, ID

ILLINOIS

A Little Spa Institute Wheeling, IL

Alvareita's College of Cosmetology Belleville, IL

Alvareita's College of Cosmetology Edwardsville, IL

Alvareita's College of Cosmetology Godfrey, IL

Cameo Beauty Academy Oak Lawn, IL

Cosmetology & Spa Institute Crystal Lake, IL

Cosmetology & Spa Institute Schaumburg, IL

Douglas J Aveda Chicago, IL

Educators of Beauty La Salle, IL

Educators of Beauty Rockford, IL

Educators of Beauty Sterling, IL

Empire Beauty School Arlington Heights Chicago Arlington Heights Chicago, IL

Empire Beauty School Hanover Park Chicago Hanover Park Chicago, IL

Empire Beauty School Stone Park Chicago Stone Park, IL

Nickee Mack

Empire Beauty School Vernon Hills Chicago Vernon Hills, IL

Empire Beauty Schools Lisle Chicago Lisle Chicago, IL

G Skin & Beauty Institute Chicago, IL

G Skin & Beauty Institute Oak Brook , IL

Hair Professionals Academy Elgin West Dundee, IL

Hair Professionals Career College Palos Hills, IL

Hair Professionals Career College Sycamore, IL

Hair Professionals School of Cosmetology Oswego, IL

Haskana Institute of Cosmetology Palatine, IL

Innovations Design Academy Canton, IL

International Academy of Makeup London Eyes, Inc. Chicago / Rosemont, IL

International Academy of Makeup London Eyes, Inc. Oakbrook Terrace, IL

International Skin Beauty Academy/ International Training Academy Chicago Area/Schaumburg, IL

John Amico School of Hair Design Oak Forest, IL

Make Up First ® School of Makeup Artistry Chicago, IL

Ms. Roberts Academy of Beauty Culture Villa Park, IL

Your Guide to a Perfect Fashion Show Production

Naperville Skin Institute Aurora Naperville, IL

New Age Spa Institute Des Plaines, IL

Niles School of Cosmetology Niles, IL

Oehrlein School of Cosmetology Peoria/Pekin/East Peoria, IL

Paul Mitchell The School Bradley Bradley, IL

Paul Mitchell The School Tinley Park Tinley Park, IL

Professional Choice Hair Design Joliet, IL

Regency Beauty Institute Aurora Naperville Aurora, IL

Regency Beauty Institute Champaign Champaign, IL

Regency Beauty Institute Crystal Lake Crystal Lake, IL

Regency Beauty Institute Darien Downers Grove Darien, IL

Regency Beauty Institute Elgin Elgin, IL

Regency Beauty Institute Fairview Heights Fairview Heights, IL

Regency Beauty Institute Joliet Joliet, IL

Regency Beauty Institute Peoria Peoria, IL

Regency Beauty Institute Rockford Rockford, IL

Regency Beauty Institute Tinley Park Tinley Park, IL

Skin Care and Spa Institute Chicago Area/Skokie, IL

Steven Papageorge Hair Academy (DBA Mac Daniel's Beauty School) Chicago, IL

Success Schools LLC Chicago, IL

The Nail Inn & School of Cosmetology Lemont, IL

The New Age Spa Institute Arlington Heights, IL

The Salon Professional Academy Elgin, IL

The Salon Professional Academy Shorewood, IL

Tricoci University of Beauty Culture Bridgeview, IL

Tricoci University of Beauty Culture Chicago NE, IL

Tricoci University of Beauty Culture Chicago NW, IL

Tricoci University of Beauty Culture Glendale Heights, IL

Tricoci University of Beauty Culture Libertyville, IL

Tricoci University of Beauty Culture Peoria, IL

Tricoci University of Beauty Culture Rockford, IL

Unity Cosmetology College Pontiac, IL

Universal Spa Training Academy Downers Grove, IL

University of Aesthetics Chicago, IL

University of Aesthetics Downers Grove, IL

University of Spa and Cosmetology Arts Springfield, IL

Vatterott College Fairview Heights Fairview Heights, IL

Vatterott College Quincy Quincy, IL

INDIANA

Empire Beauty School Indianapolis Indianapolis, IN

Empire Beauty School Indianapolis Speedway Indianapolis Speedway, IN

Lafayette Beauty Academy Lafayette, IN

Michiana Beauty College Granger, IN

Regency Beauty Institute Avon Indianapolis Avon, IN

Regency Beauty Institute Castleton Indianapolis Castleton, IN

Regency Beauty Institute Evansville Evansville, IN

Regency Beauty Institute Greenwood Indianapolis Greenwood, IN

Regency Beauty Institute Merrillville Merrillville, IN

Regency Beauty Institute South Bend South Bend, IN

Roger's Academy of Hair Evansville, IN

Roger's Hair Academy (East) Evansville, IN

Success Barber School Merrillville, IN

The Salon Professional Academy, Anderson, IN

The Salon Professional Academy, Kokomo, IN

Tricoci University of Beauty, Culture Highland, IN

Tricoci University of Beauty Culture, formerly Honors Beauty College, Indianapolis NE, IN

IOWA

American Hair Academy, formerly Bill Hill's College of Cosmetology, Fort Madison, IA

Aveda Institute Des Moines, Des Moines (West), IA

Capri College, Cedar Rapids, IA

Capri College, Davenport, IA

Capri College, Dubuque, IA

Paul Mitchell The School Davenport, Davenport , IA

The Salon Professional Academy, Iowa City, IA

KANSAS

Academy of Aesthetic Arts Shawnee, KS

Bellus Academy Manhattan, KS

Entourage Institute of Beauty and Esthetics Lenexa, KS

Eric Fisher Academy Wichita, KS

LaBaron Hairdressing Academy, Overland Park, KS

Marinello Schools of Beauty, formerly B Street Design School of International Hair Styling, Lawrence , KS

Marinello Schools of Beauty, formerly B Street Design School of International Hair Styling, Manhattan, KS

Marinello Schools of Beauty, formerly B Street Design School of International Hair Styling Overland Park, KS

Marinello Schools of Beauty, formerly B Street Design School of International Hair Styling Topeka, KS

Marinello Schools of Beauty, formerly B Street Design School of International Hair Styling Wichita, KS

Regency Beauty Institute Olathe Olathe, KS

Regency Beauty Institute Topeka Topeka, KS

Regency Beauty Institute Wichita Wichita, KS

KENTUCKY

Empire Beauty School Elizabethtown Fort Knox Elizabethtown Fort Knox, KY

Empire Beauty School Florence Cincinnati Florence Cincinnati, KY

Empire Beauty School Louisville Chenoweth Louisville Chenoweth, KY

Empire Beauty School Louisville Dixie Highway Louisville Dixie Highway, KY

Empire Beauty School Louisville Highland Louisville Highland, KY

Empire Beauty School Louisville Hurstbourne Louisville Hurstbourne, KY

The Salon Professional Academy Lexington, KY

LOUISIANA

Aveda Institute Baton Rouge Baton Rouge, LA

Aveda Institute Covington Covington, LA

Aveda Institute Lafayette Lafayette, LA

Aveda Institute New Orleans Metairie, LA

Career Technical College (CTC) Shreveport, LA

Regency Beauty Institute Shreveport Shreveport, LA

Remington College Baton Rouge Baton Rouge, LA

Remington College Lafayette, LA

Virginia College Baton Rouge Baton Rouge, LA

Virginia College Shreveport Shreveport, LA

MAINE

Cosmotech School of Cosmetology Portland, ME

Empire Beauty School Bangor Bangor, ME

Empire Beauty School Caribou Presque Isle Caribou Presque Isle, ME

Empire Beauty School Portland Portland, ME

Empire Beauty School Waterville Augusta Waterville Augusta, ME

Spa Tech Institute Westbrook, ME

MARYLAND

Aesthetics Institute of Cosmetology Gaithersburg, MD

American Beauty Academy Baltimore, MD

American Beauty Academy Wheaton, MD

Aspen Beauty Academy of Laurel Laurel, MD

Award Beauty School Hagerstown, MD

Baltimore School of Massage's Steiner Institute of Esthetics Linthicum, MD

Blades School of Hair Design California, MD

Empire Beauty School Glen Burnie Baltimore Glen Burnie, MD

Empire Beauty School Owings Mills Baltimore Owings Mills Baltimore, MD

Fortis Institute Woodlawn Woodlawn, MD

Hair Academy II Suitland , MD

Hair Academy New Carrollton, MD

Hair Expressions Academy A Paul Mitchell Partner School Rockville, MD

Montgomery Beauty School Silver Spring, MD

Park West Barber School Baltimore, MD

Paul Mitchell the School Jessup Jessup, MD

Regency Beauty Institute Baltimore Baltimore, MD

Regency Beauty Institute Gaithersburg Gaithersburg, MD

Von Lee International School of Aesthetics, Inc. Baltimore, MD

MASSACHUSETTS

Catherine Hinds Institute Boston Metro/Woburn , MA

Central Mass School of Massage & Therapy Spencer, MA

Your Guide to a Perfect Fashion Show Production

Cosmix School of Beauty Sciences Marlborough, MA

Elizabeth Grady School of Esthetics Medford, MA

Empire Beauty School Boston, MA

Empire Beauty School Framingham, Boston, MA

Empire Beauty School Hyannis, MA

Empire Beauty School Lowell Boston, MA

Empire Beauty School Malden Boston, MA

Jolie Health and Beauty Academy Ludlow, MA

Kay Harvey Hairdressing Academy West Springfield, MA

LaBaron Hairdressing Academy Brockton, MA

LaBaron Hairdressing Academy New Bedford, MA

Mansfield Beauty Schools Quincy, MA

Mansfield Beauty Schools Springfield, MA

Marinello Schools of Beauty, formerly Brio Academy Northampton, MA

New England Hair Academy Malden, MA

Spa Tech Institute Ipswich, MA

Spa Tech Institute Plymouth, MA

Spa Tech Institute Westboro, MA

TONI & GUY Hairdressing Academy Braintree, MA

TONI & GUY Hairdressing Academy Central Massachusetts/Worcester, MA

MICHIGAN

Douglas J Aveda Institute Ann Arbor, MI

Douglas J Aveda Institute East Lansing, MI

Douglas J Aveda Institute Grand Rapids, MI

Empire Beauty School Grand Rapids East Grand Rapids East, MI

Empire Beauty School Grand Rapids Walker Grand Rapids Walker , MI

Empire Beauty School Portage Kalamazoo Portage Kalamazoo, MI

Gallery College of Beauty Clinton Township, MI

Marketti Academy of Cosmetology Waterford, MI

Michigan College of Beauty A Pivot Point Career Center Troy, MI

Regency Beauty Institute Detroit Lakeside Shelby Township, MI

Regency Beauty Institute Flint Flint, MI

Regency Beauty Institute Grand Rapids Grand Rapids, MI

Regency Beauty Institute Lansing Lansing, MI

The Salon Academy Coldwater, MI

Traverse City Beauty College Traverse City, MI

Tulip City Beauty College Holland, MI

Twin City Beauty College Saint Joseph, MI

MINNESOTA

Avalon School of Cosmetology Worthington, MN

Cosmetology Careers Unlimited Duluth, MN

Cosmetology Careers Unlimited Hibbing, MN

Empire Beauty School Bloomington Bloomington, MN

Empire Beauty School Brooklyn Park Fridley Brooklyn Park Fridley, MN

Empire Beauty School Eden Prairie Hopkins Eden Prairie Hopkins, MN

Empire Beauty School St. Paul St. Paul, MN

Hastings Beauty School, Inc. Hastings, MN

Minnesota School of Cosmetology Plymouth, MN

Minnesota School of Cosmetology Woodbury, MN

Model College of Hair Design Saint Cloud, MN

Nova Academy of Cosmetology Rochester, MN

Regency Beauty Institute Blaine Blaine, MN

Regency Beauty Institute Burnsville Burnsville, MN

Regency Beauty Institute Duluth Duluth, MN

Regency Beauty Institute Maplewood Maplewood, MN

Regency Beauty Institute Ridgedale Ridgedale, MN

Regency Beauty Institute St. Cloud St. Cloud, MN

MISSISSIPPI

Delta Technical College

Virginia College at Jackson Jackson, MS

Virginia College Biloxi Biloxi, MS

MISSOURI

Academy of Hair Design Springfield, MO

Grabber School of Hair Design and Nail Technology Ballwin, MO

Heritage College Kansas City, MO

House of Heavilin Beauty College Blue Springs, MO

House of Heavilin Beauty College Kansas City, MO

House of Heavilin Beauty College Raymore, MO

Regency Beauty Institute Independence Independence, MO

Regency Beauty Institute Mehlville Mehlville, MO

Regency Beauty Institute Springfield Springfield, MO

Regency Beauty Institute St. Peters St Peters, MO

The Salon Professional Academy St. Charles, MO

Vatterott College Berkeley Berkeley, MO

Vatterott College Joplin Campus Joplin, MO

Vatterott College Kansas City Kansas City, MO

Vatterott College St. Charles St. Charles, MO

Vatterott College St. Joseph Campus St. Joseph, MO

Xenon International Academy A Pivot Point Member School Ballwin / St Louis Metro, MO

MONTANA

Academy of Nail, Skin & Hair, Inc. Billings, MT

The Salon Professional Academy Great Falls, MT

NEBRASKA

Joseph's College Beatrice, NE

Joseph's College Grand Island, NE

Joseph's College Hastings, NE

Joseph's College Kearney, NE

Joseph's College Lincoln, NE

Joseph's College Norfolk, NE

Joseph's College North Platte, NE

Vatterott College at Omaha Omaha Spring Valley, NE

NEVADA

Academy of Hair Design

Aveda Institute Vegas

G Skin and Beauty Institute

Milan Institute of Cosmetology

NEW HAMPSHIRE

Empire Beauty Schools of New Hampshire

Michael's Beauty School, A Paul Mitchell Partner School

Paul Mitchell The School Portsmouth

NEW JERSEY

Artistic Academy of Hair Design Morris Plains, NJ

CAPRI Institute, Cosmetology Training Centers Clifton, NJ

Christine Valmy International School of Esthetics and Cosmetology Pine Brook, NJ

Cutting Edge Academy Roxbury, NJ

Empire Beauty School Bordentown Trenton Bordentown Trenton, NJ

Empire Beauty School Cherry Hill Cherry Hill, NJ

Empire Beauty School Laurel Springs Clementon Laurel Springs Clementon, NJ

Empire Beauty School Paramus Paramus, NJ

Jolie Health and Beauty Academy Northfield, NJ

P.B. Cosmetology Education Centre Gloucester, NJ

Parisian Beauty Academy Paul Mitchell Partner School Hackensack, NJ

Robert Fiance Beauty Schools Gloucester County, NJ

Robert Fiance Beauty Schools North Plainfield, NJ

Robert Fiance Beauty Schools Perth Amboy, NJ

Robert Fiance Beauty Schools West New York, NJ

Robert Fiance Makeup Academy Perth Amboy, NJ

Shore Beauty School Egg Harbor Township, NJ

The Bond Academy Bloomfield, NJ

The Hair Design School Bloomfield East Orange Bloomfield East Orange, NJ

The Hair Design School Jersey City Jersey City, NJ

The Hair Design School Ocean Township Asbury/Park Ocean Township Asbury Park, NJ

The Hair Design School Union Newark Union Newark, NJ

The Lab Paul Mitchell Partner School Ewing, NJ

The Salon Professional Academy South Plainfield, NJ

NORTH CAROLINA

Aveda Institute Chapel Hill

Aveda Institute Charlotte

Empire Beauty School - Charlotte-Concord

Empire Beauty School - Charlotte-Pineville

Empire Beauty School - West-Greensboro

Miller-Motte College – Fayetteville

Miller-Motte College – Greenville

Miller-Motte College – Jacksonville

Miller-Motte College – Raleigh

Miller-Motte College – Wilmington

Paul Mitchell the School-Gastonia

Regency Beauty Institute – Charlotte

Regency Beauty Institute – Durham

Regency Beauty Institute - Winston-Salem

The Hair Design School – Charlotte

The Hair Design School – Greensboro

The Hair Design School - Winston-Salem

Virginia College-Greensboro

NORTH DAKOTA

Josef's School of Hair Design-Downtown Campus

Josef's West Academy

The Salon Professional Academy

OHIO

Aveda Institute Columbus Columbus, OH

Brown Aveda Institute Cleveland/Rocky River, OH

Brown Aveda Institute Mentor, OH

Casal Aveda Institute Austintown, OH

Cincinnati Academy Paul Mitchell Partner School Cincinnati, OH

Creative Images Institute of Cosmetology Dayton (North) Dayton , OH

Creative Images Institute of Cosmetology Dayton (South) Dayton , OH

Empire Beauty School Cincinnati Cincinnati, OH

Miami Jacobs Career College Springboro, OH

Miami Jacobs Career College Troy, OH

Nationwide Beauty Academy & Spa Studio Hilliard, OH

Ohio State School of Cosmetology Heath Heath, OH

Ohio State Schools of Cosmetology Africentric Program Columbus, OH

Ohio State Schools of Cosmetology Canal Winchester, OH

Ohio State Schools of Cosmetology Westerville Westerville, OH

Regency Beauty Institute Akron Akron, OH

Regency Beauty Institute Canton Canton, OH

Regency Beauty Institute Cincinnati / Eastgate Cincinnati (East), OH

Regency Beauty Institute Cincinnati / Tri County Cincinnati / Tri County, OH

Regency Beauty Institute Cleveland Cleveland Willoughby, OH

Regency Beauty Institute Columbus Columbus, OH

Regency Beauty Institute Dayton Dayton, OH

Regency Beauty Institute North Olmsted North Olmsted, OH

Regency Beauty Institute Toledo Holland, OH

Remington College Cleveland Cleveland, OH

The Hair Experts Barber School Canal Winchester, OH

The Ohio Academy Paul Mitchell Partner School Twinsburg, OH

The Salon Professional Academy Cincinnati Cincinnati, OH

The Salon Professional Academy Perrysburg, OH

The Spa School Columbus, OH

Toledo Academy of Beauty Culture (East) Oregon, OH

TONI&GUY Hairdressing Academy Toledo, OH

Vanity School of Cosmetology Middleburg Heights , OH

OKLAHOMA

Central State Beauty and Wellness College

Enid Beauty College Inc

I.T.S. Academy of Beauty

Imagine Paul Mitchell Partner School

OREGON

IBS School of Cosmetology

Phagans Salon Academy

Phagans' School of Hair Design

PENNSYLVANIA

A Metro Beauty Academy

Altoona Beauty School

Bucks County School of Beauty Culture

Chambersburg Beauty & Barber School

Empire Beauty School - Allentown-Whitehall

Empire Beauty School – Hanover

Empire Beauty School – Harrisburg

Empire Beauty School – Lancaster

Your Guide to a Perfect Fashion Show Production

Empire Beauty School – Lebanon

Empire Beauty School - Monroeville-Pittsburgh

Empire Beauty School - Moosic-Wilkes Barre-Scranton

Empire Beauty School - Philadelphia – Cheltenham

Empire Beauty School - Philadelphia-Center City

Empire Beauty School - Philadelphia-Northeast

Empire Beauty School - Pittsburgh-North Hills

Empire Beauty School – Pottsville

Empire Beauty School – Reading

Empire Beauty School - Shamokin Dam-Sunbury

Fortis Institute-Erie

Jolie Health and Beauty Academy

Lancaster School of Cosmetology

Laurel Technical Institute

The Beauty Institute - Schwarzkopf Professional – Allentown

The Beauty Institute, Schwarzkopf Professional – Ambler

The Beauty Institute, Schwarzkopf Professional – Philadelphia

The Cosmetology Academy at Douglas Education Center

The Salon Professional Academy, formerly Pruontos Hair Design Institute

Toni&Guy Hairdressing Academy – Erie

Venus Beauty Academy

Schools in Rhode Island with Cosmetology Programs

Empire Beauty School – Warwick Warwick, RI

SOUTH CAROLINA

Kenneth Shuler's School of Cosmetology

Miller-Motte Technical College – Charleston

Miller-Motte Technical College – Conway

Regency Beauty Institute – Columbia

Remington College – Columbia

Virginia College-Charleston

Virginia College-Columbia

SOUTH DAKOTA

Desaree & Company School of Beauty – Sturgis, SD

Your Guide to a Perfect Fashion Show Production

TENNESSEE

Aveda Institute Nashville

Empire Beauty Schools - Brentwood-Nashville

Empire Beauty Schools - Memphis

Georgia Career Institute (TN)

Georgia Career Institute Murfreesboro

Miller-Motte Technical College - Chattanooga

Miller-Motte Technical College - Clarksville

Mister Wayne's Beauty & Barber

Regency Beauty Institute - Chattanooga

Regency Beauty Institute - Knoxville

Regency Beauty Institute - Nashville

Regency Beauty Institute - North Nashville

Tennessee Career Institute

The Hair Design School - Jackson

The Hair Design School - Memphis-Coleman Road

The Hair Design School - Memphis-Highland

Virginia College at Chattanooga

Virginia College-Knoxville

TEXAS

Aveda Institute Austin Austin, TX

Aveda Institute Dallas Dallas, TX

Aveda Institute Houston Shenandoah, TX

Avenue Five Institute Austin, TX

Bella Institute of Permanent Cosmetics Fort Worth, TX

Duvall's School of Cosmetology Bedford, TX

Exposito School of Hair Design Amarillo, TX

I.T.S. Academy of Beauty Arlington, TX

I.T.S. Academy of Beauty Denton, TX

I.T.S. Academy of Beauty El Paso, TX

I.T.S. Academy of Beauty Fort Worth, TX

I.T.S. Academy of Beauty Hurst, TX

I.T.S. Academy of Beauty Irving, TX

I.T.S. Academy of Beauty Lewisville, TX

I.T.S. Academy of Beauty Mesquite, TX

I.T.S. Academy of Beauty Plano, TX

Your Guide to a Perfect Fashion Show Production

I.T.S. Academy of Beauty Wichita Falls, TX

Milan Institute of Cosmetology Amarillo, TX

Milan Institute of Cosmetology El Paso El Paso, TX

Milan Institute of Cosmetology San Antonio (South), TX

Milan Institute of Cosmetology San Antonio (Windcrest), TX

Milan Institute San Antonio (Ingram Park), TX

Natural Images Beauty College Clute, TX

Nuvani Institute North (S.W. School of Business & Technical Career) Austin, TX

Nuvani Institute South (S.W. School of Business & Technical Career) Austin, TX

Ogle School of Hair Skin Nails Arlington, TX

Ogle School of Hair Skin Nails Dallas, TX

Ogle School of Hair Skin Nails Fort Worth, TX

Ogle School of Hair Skin Nails Hurst, TX

Ogle School of Hair Skin Nails North Dallas, TX

Ogle School of Hair Skin Nails San Antonio, TX

Ogle School of Hair, Skin, and Nails Denton, TX

Ogle School of Hair, Skin, and Nails Houston Stafford, TX

Quest College San Antonio, TX

Regency Beauty Institute Arlington Arlington, TX

Regency Beauty Institute Austin Austin, TX

Regency Beauty Institute Austin Round Rock Austin Round Rock, TX

Regency Beauty Institute Collin Creek Collin Creek, TX

Regency Beauty Institute Copperwood Houston Northwest, TX

Regency Beauty Institute Cypresswood Houston Cypresswood, TX

Regency Beauty Institute Dallas Galleria Dallas, TX

Regency Beauty Institute El Paso El Paso, TX

Regency Beauty Institute Lewisville Lewisville, TX

Regency Beauty Institute Mesquite Mesquite, TX

Regency Beauty Institute Pasadena Houston Southeast, TX

Regency Beauty Institute San Antonio San Antonio, TX

Remington College Dallas (Garland) Dallas Area / Garland, TX

Remington College Houston (Westchase) Houston, TX

Remington College Houston Southeast (Webster) Webster, TX

Remington College North Houston (Greenspoint) Houston, TX

Salon Boutique Academy Addison, TX

Tint School of Makeup and Cosmetology Dallas, TX

Tint School of Makeup and Cosmetology Grand Prairie, TX

Tint School of Makeup and Cosmetology Irving, TX

TONI&GUY Academy Dallas , TX

Total Transformation Institute of Cosmetology San Marcos, TX

Vista College Killeen, TX

Vista College Lubbock, TX

UTAH

Avalon School of Cosmetology Layton, UT

Aveda Institute Provo Provo, UT

Cameo College of Essential Beauty Murray, UT

Echelon Edge Academy of Hair, Skin and Nails Sandy, UT

ImageWorks Academy of Hair Design Spanish Fork, UT

Mandalyn Academy American Fork, UT

Marinello Schools of Beauty Layton, UT

Marinello Schools of Beauty Ogden, UT

Marinello Schools of Beauty Provo, UT

National Institute of Medical Aesthetics South Jordan, UT

Paul Mitchell the School Ogden Ogden , UT

Paul Mitchell the School Salt Lake City Salt Lake City, UT

Paul Mitchell the School St George Washington, UT

Sherman Kendall's Academy Fort Union Midvale, UT

Sherman Kendall's Academy Sugarhouse Salt Lake City, UT

Skin Science Institute Orem, UT

Skin Science Institute Salt Lake City, UT

Steiner Institute of Esthetics at UCMT Salt Lake City, UT

VERMONT

Aveda Institute Williston

Bella Capelli

Empire Beauty Schools

New England School of Hair Design

Your Guide to a Perfect Fashion Show Production

O'Briens Aveda Institute, So. Burlington, VT

VIRGINIA

Empire Beauty School - Midlothian-Richmond

Empire Beauty School – Richmond

Empire Beauty School - Virginia-Beach

Miller-Motte Technical College – Roanoke

Regency Beauty Institute – Manassas

Regency Beauty Institute - Newport News

Regency Beauty Institute – Roanoke

Suffolk Beauty Academy

Sylvain Melloul International Hair Academy

Virginia College-Richmond

WASHINGTON

Bellevue Beauty School (now Evergreen Beauty College) Bellevue, WA

Evergreen Beauty College Everett, WA

Gary Manuel AVEDA Institute Seattle, WA

Gene Juarez Academy Federal Way, WA

Gene Juarez Academy Seattle, WA

Lucas Marc Academy Richland, WA

Paroba College Everett, WA

TONI&GUY Hairdressing Academy Bellingham, WA

TONI&GUY Hairdressing Academy Shoreline, WA

WEST VIRGINIA

Clarksburg Beauty Academy, WV

LBI School of Cosmetology

Morgantown

Morgantown Beauty College

WISCONSIN

Academy of Advanced Esthetics, LLC Janesville, WI

AVEDA Institute VICI Madison Madison, WI

AVEDA Institute VICI Milwaukee Milwaukee, WI

Cosmetology Careers Unlimited , WI

Empire Beauty School Appleton Menasha Appleton Menasha, WI

Empire Beauty School Green Bay Green Bay, WI

Empire Beauty School Madison Madison, WI

Empire Beauty School Manitowoc Two Rivers Manitowoc Two Rivers, WI

Empire Beauty School Milwaukee Milwaukee, WI

Gill Tech Academy of Hair Design Appleton, WI

Regency Beauty Institute Greenfield Milwaukee, WI

Regency Beauty Institute Madison Madison, WI

State College of Beauty Culture, Wausau, WI

The Academy Waukesha Paul Mitchell Partner School, Waukesha, WI

The Institute of Beauty and Wellness (Aveda School), Milwaukee, WI

The Salon Professional Academy, Kenosha, WI

VICI Beauty School, Milwaukee, WI

WYOMING

Academy of Cosmetology

Advanced College of Cosmetology

Aveda Institute Madison

Aveda IBW

Nickee Mack

Empire Beauty School

First Class Cosmetology School

Gill-Tech Academy

Paul Mitchell The School Green Bay

Paul Mitchell The School Milwaukee

Paul Mitchell The School Monroe

Regency Beauty Institute – Greenfield

State College-Beauty Culture

VICÍ Beauty Schools - Milwaukee Campus

About the Author

MsNickee Mack is a seasoned industry professional with more than 10 years of experience emphasizing team leadership methods, recognizing the importance of high-quality and targeted content, and ethical networking. She is an expert at building productions for clients ranging from solopreneurs to Fortune 500 companies.

As a professional in the hair, beauty, and fashion industry who is educated, certified and still growing, she works consistently in the industry with like-minded individuals to help build their brands as well as her own. MsNickee is also the show producer for various clients, a brand ambassador for several brands, and represents models in their reign as ambassadors and signature models for various clients.

This lady wears the hats of runway coach, image consultant, social media brand manager, licensed esthetician, published makeup artist, show producer, model coordinator, agent, show and event host, and comprehensive hair, beauty and fashion expert! From her very own words to this page, MsNickee unflinchingly shares just who *MsNickee* is . . .

> *"I am a self- proclaimed workaholic, and I make no apologies for it. I do what I love and I love what I do. This business is my life, and I plan to continue to do it for the rest of my life!"*

Nickee Mack

MsNickee is truly a 21st Century extraordinary entrepreneur who is on the horizon of being a legend in her own right. Her character and attention to excellence far exceeds what most people have not yet acquired.

It has been my experience in working with her that she has the ability to not be selfish and has accepted the calling of helping others. She has learned the lesson that few obtain in her profession that . . . **"If I help someone else achieve their dream, then it shall certainly come back to my turn."** Greatness lies in her as she travels this road called DESTINY.

BISHOP, DR. DEBRA W. MCALPINE
FOUNDER AND CEO OF DESTINY INCEPTION

MsNickee has also hosted, produced and been a part of several high-profile shows and events over the years, such as appearing on Lifetime Television, FFFWeek, Trumpet Awards, Legendary Awards, NYFW, VH1's R&B Divas, 11Alive News, Jacksonville Fox 5 News, Spokesperson for Outre (a multi-billion dollars hair company), FSO Atlanta, Bronner Brother, ORS (Olive Oil Brand)—and the list could go on and on. Hosting events, choreography, and show productions are just more elements that make up this wonderfully huge personality that will expand all across the globe because of her multifaceted dynamics. This plus model turned hair, beauty and fashion mogul chooses to change the face of the industry one step at a time, with positive, strong, determined individuals who are focused and destined for greatness.

www.ingramcontent.com/pod-product-compliance
Lightning Source LLC
Chambersburg PA
CBHW060352190526
45169CB00002B/570